Beautiful as You

Overcome Negative Self Talk God's Way

Devotional & Prayer Journal

For Christian Women

— Jenny L. Kessel —

I dedicate this journal to my husband, John, for always supporting my dreams.

and

To my daughter, Izabel, that she may always know her true value.

The Thoughts and Prayers Of

Table of Contents

Letter to the Reader

Dear Beautiful Friend,

I believe it is no mistake that you are holding this book in your hands right now. In fact, I prayed for you to be led here; that God would speak clearly to you of how loved you are.

For many years, I felt stuck, trapped, and that my life was just not worth living. I often wondered who would even miss me, convinced I was a mistake. Of course, I know now those were all lies straight from the enemy. Satan did everything he could do to keep me down, depressed, and hopeless. I believe depression and anxiety are two of his best moves to keep us from the beautiful blessings God has for us.

But God had big plans for me, and he does for you, too! Even when I was so low that the only cry out to God that I could barely muster was *Jesus, help me*, he stepped in and pulled me from the ashes. He rewrote my story and made me whole again. This is just what he does; He brings beauty for ashes, restores joy, and releases us from the sorrow that has kept us in bondage.

My stories of personal struggle are included to remind you that we all have sin. Yours may look different than mine, but we both have the opportunity for forgiveness by calling upon the Lord. We don't have to wallow or live in that sin; we can overcome it through the salvation Jesus Christ offers us.

The journaling prompts are designed to help you work through sin or pain you are holding on to. The intent is for you to move from what is keeping you stagnant to accepting forgiveness and moving forward. I encourage you to thoughtfully consider your responses for best results.

I am elated you are about to begin this journey of transformation! I just can't wait for you to see what the Lord is getting ready to do in your heart. Hold on, sister. It's going to be an incredible ride!

With Love and Hugs,

Jenny K

How To Use This Journal

For 21 Days

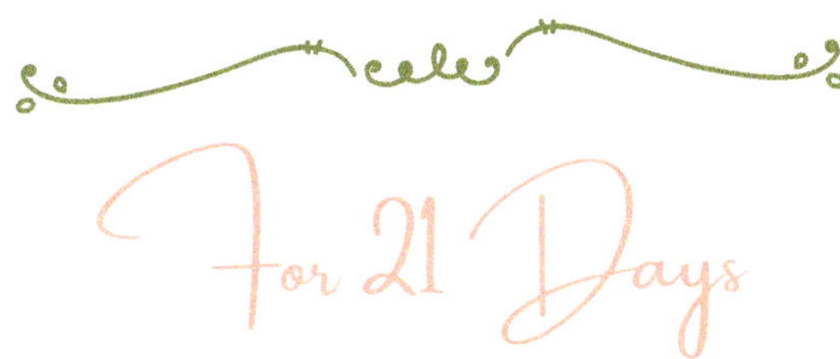

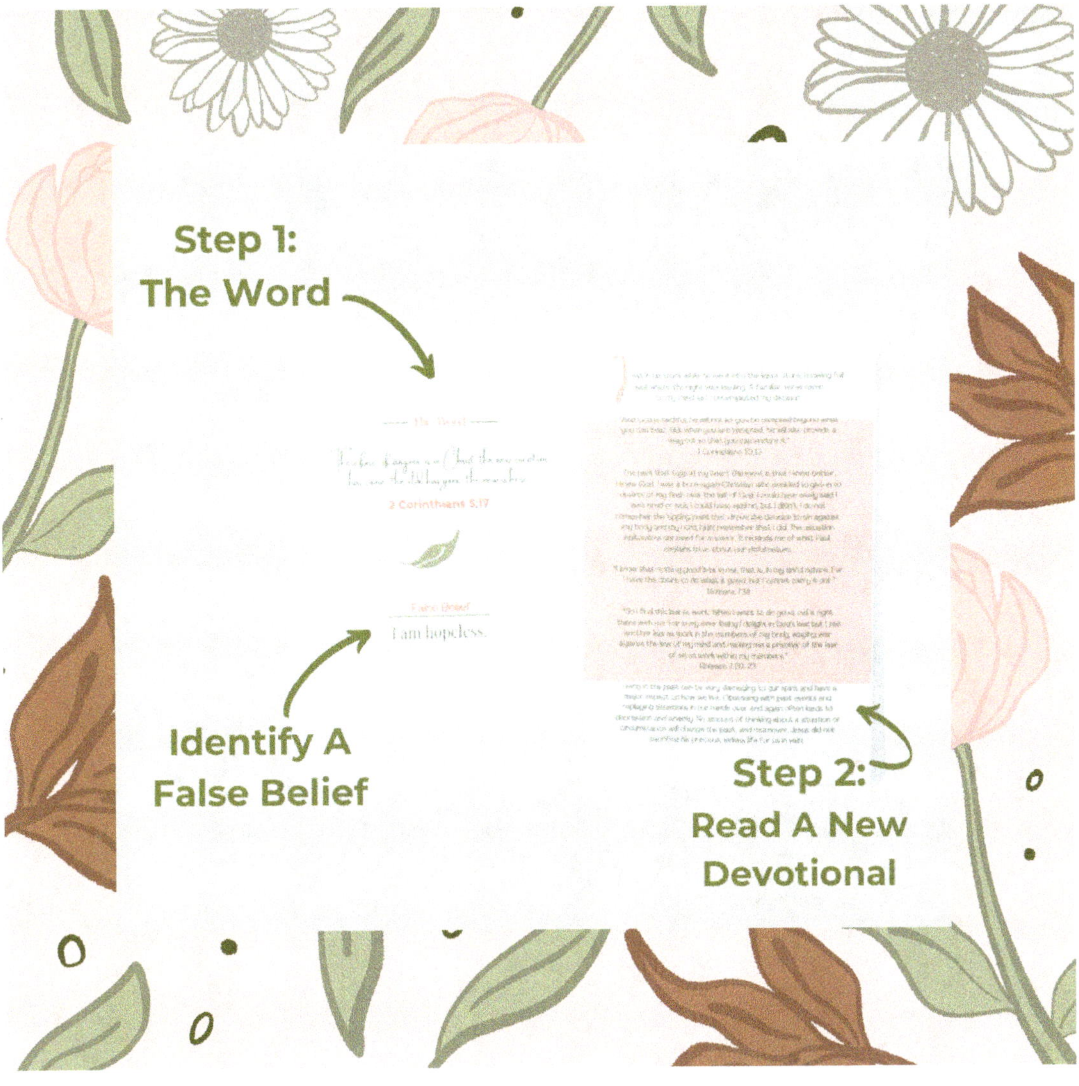
Step 1:
The Word
2 Corinthians 5:17
I am hopeless.
Identify A
False Belief
Step 2:
Read A New
Devotional

Step 3:
Say A Prayer

Step 4:
Speak And Write A New Positive Affirmation

**Visit
https://bit.ly/JournalPagesandCards
for extra journal pages,
and printable affirmations
to keep with you each day.**

**Step 5:
Journal Your
Thoughts And Prayers
With New Prompts**

Day One

I Am a New Creation

Therefore, if anyone is in Christ, the new creation has come: the old has gone, the new is here.

2 Corinthians 5:17

False Belief

I am hopeless.

I sat in his truck while he went into the liquor store, knowing full well where the night was leading. A familiar verse came to my mind as I contemplated my decision.

"And God is faithful; he will not let you be tempted beyond what you can bear. But when you are tempted, he will also provide a way out so that you can endure it."
1 Corinthians 10:13

The part that tugs at my heart the most is that I knew better, I knew God. I was a born-again Christian who decided to give in to desires of my flesh over the will of God. I could have easily said I was tired or sick, I could have said no, but I didn't. I do not remember the tipping point that drove the decision to sin against my body and my Lord, I just remember that I did. This situation epitomizes our need for a savior. It reminds me of what Paul explains to us about our sinful nature.

"I know that nothing good lives in me, that is, in my sinful nature. For I have the desire to do what is good, but I cannot carry it out."
Romans 7:18

"So I find this law at work: When I want to do good, evil is right there with me. For in my inner being I delight in God's law; but I see another law at work in the members of my body, waging war against the law of my mind and making me a prisoner of the law of sin at work within my members."
Romans 7:20-23

Living in the past can be very damaging to our spirit and have a major impact on how we live. Obsessing with past events and replaying situations in our minds over and again often leads to depression and anxiety. No amount of thinking about a situation or circumstance will change the past, and moreover, Jesus did not sacrifice his precious, sinless life for us in vain.

He came so we could live to the fullest measure, free from fear, worry, and condemnation. He died that we might have eternal life with him.

"The thief comes only to steal and kill and destroy; I have come that they may have life, and have it to the full."
John 10:10

Because of our trust in Christ, we do not need to scrutinize our past. His monumental sacrifice eradicates sins from our lives and deems them forever absolved! We have a clean slate with nothing to cloud our vision and our walk with him. As freeing as this is, this truth can be a tough one to grasp, and Satan knows this. He will do everything he can to convince us to keep a tight grip on our pasts. God wants us to let it go, trust Jesus Christ as our savior, and accept the gift of his grace.

"Therefore, there is now no condemnation for those who are in Christ Jesus, because through Christ Jesus the law of the Spirit who gives life has set you free from the law of sin and death." Romans 8:1-2

Becoming a new creation does not mean we will no longer sin. We are sinful by nature as forementioned; sin is inevitable. Don't let that burden you...there is a silver lining! Our belief in Christ Jesus as Lord means all of our sins past, present, and future are forgotten when we ask for his forgiveness. We receive a new heart posture that desires to turn away from sin and ultimately with the help of the Holy Spirit, we begin to look more like Christ.

"If we confess our sins, he is faithful and just and will forgive us our sins and purify us from all unrighteousness." 1 John 1:9

Scripture References:

2 Corinthians 5:17, 1 Corinthians 10:13, Romans 7:18, Romans 7:20-23, John 10:10, Romans 8:1-2, 1 John 1:9

Thank you for your son. Jesus. Because of him. I am made new and do not consider anything in the past. Thank you. Lord. that I am free from my sins because of his sacrifice on the cross for me. Help me today so I do not let my thoughts wander to sins from my former life. Let my focus be on the new creation in me that you continue to sanctify.

Replace It!

When lies enter your thoughts today,
immediately replace them with...

" I Am a New Creation "

Write It!

I am a

new creation

What are you holding
on to that Jesus has
already forgiven?

What will it
take for you
to let that go
and receive
God's grace?
What false belief
will you let go
of today?

Day Two

I Am a Child of God

"Yet to all who did receive him, to those who believed in his name, he gave the right to become children of God."

John 1:2

False Belief

I don't fit in.

As a preteen, I remember feeling lost and I did not seem to fit anywhere. I was taller, bigger, more prone to acne than the other girls in my grade, and ungainly. Rebellion to this was to become a tomboy, my way of communicating to the world that I did not care to fit in.

Excelling in sports made my family proud but I resented the negative attention it brought me from older kids at school. I developed a false belief very early in life … People don't like you when you are better than them at things.

Instead of praise, love, and support from my peers, I was bullied, made fun of, and pushed out by the older girls who did not appreciate someone younger taking a spot on their team. This was traumatic for a young girl and spiraled into a desperation of trying to please others and fit in. I avoided the spotlight and dropped out of the things I enjoyed and was good at.

"For our light and momentary troubles are achieving for us an eternal glory that far outweighs them all."
2 Corinthians 4:17

Later, in my teens and on into my early twenties, I looked to the attention and affection from boys as a way to find acceptance and love. Looking back, it was an attempt to be validated as a person and the need to matter. All attempts fell short of the actual truth about myself that I so longed to hear and believe. Not knowing this at the time, I needed someone to pour into me the love of God and all the ways I matter to him.

I catch myself worrying about challenges my daughter may face in the future. I want her to know she has a place in our family that will always be and more importantly, in God's family. As my child and a child of God, she will always be enough, always be loved, and always be accepted just the way she was created.

"Train a child in the way he should go, and when he is old he
will not turn from it." Proverbs 22:6

Some may have a family that is loving, supportive, and always in their
corner; I know families like this, and it's a beautiful thing to observe.
Some may not know this level of support and acceptance. No matter
what the situation looks like here in this temporary life, our heavenly
home awaits us where all God's children fit perfectly.

"The Spirit himself testifies with our spirit that we are God's children."
Romans 8:16

Father, help me to remember whose child I am: that I am your daughter and you love me... so much so, you sent your son to die for me so I can be with you forever. Thank you that I get to be a part of your family forever. Please help me to forgive those who have hurt me in the past. Please heal any deep wounds that are still open and cause me to have false beliefs.

In Jesus' name, amen.

Replace It!

When lies enter your thoughts today,
immediately replace them with...

"I Am a Child of God."

Write It!

Think back to a time when you felt like you did not fit in. How has the impact of that experience resurfaced later in your life?

In contrast, how does it feel knowing that you always fit in as a child of God?

What false belief will you let go of today?

Day Three

I Am God's Workmanship, His Handiwork

" For We are God's handiwork, created in Christ Jesus to do good works which God prepared in advance for us to do."

Ephesians 2:10

False Belief

I am a mistake.

nything but me, Lord, can you change me to be anything but me? With a tear-streaked face, I begged the Lord to change who he created me to be. Can you imagine the clay telling the potter that he shaped it wrong?

"Woe to those who quarrel with their Maker, those who are nothing but potsherds among the potsherds on the ground. Does the clay say to the potter, 'What are you making?' Does your work say, 'The potter has no hands'?"
Isaiah 45:9

Satan brought my focus to all the ways that I am not like the others in my circle. His questions were daunting, and they planted seeds that rooted deep in my innermost being for many years.

Why do you get nervous in crowds? Why aren't you laughing like everyone else? Why are you so serious? Why do you like to be alone so much? Why are you so weird, odd, fat, and ugly? Why doesn't your nose line up with your mouth, and why do you sound so funny? WHY?

"Be alert and of sober mind. Your enemy the devil prowls around like a roaring lion looking for someone to devour."
1 Peter 5:8

My thoughts were consumed with coveting the traits of others that kept me from seeing the masterpiece that I am. Wishing to be prettier like Erika, thinner like Elizabeth, funnier like Jenny, wittier like Katharine, and bolder like Angela, etc. I did not realize at the time that I was actually perfect for the plans he had prepared for me.

"Yet you, Lord, are our Father. We are the clay, you are the potter; we are all the work of your hand."
Isaiah 64:8

It's taken much prayer and self-work to move away from that bondage of self-loathing. Still, it creeps back every now and again. The difference now is that I recognize it as lies and can squash it before it starts to take over my head space. My new response is to immediately renounce it and then I have a visualization that makes me smile every time. Picture God as the potter working his hands around the clay and forming his masterpiece. I love to imagine that I am the handiwork he is so creatively crafting into existence.

He determined our skin, hair, and eye color, shaped our eyes, nose, and mouth. He handed out to each of us specific traits and details that no one else shares. How incredible! How marvelous that when we look in the mirror each day we are looking at what God has called "good." We look, act, and sound the way he designed us even before we were born! How could we ever wish to be different knowing he designed every fiber of our being? We are equipped explicitly with what we need to carry out the purpose he has for us.

"For I know the plans I have for you," declares the Lord, "plans to prosper you and not to harm you, plans to give you hope and a future. Then you will call on me and come and pray to me, and I will listen to you. You will seek me and find me when you seek me with all your heart." Jeremiah 29: 11-13

Father, forgive me for all the times I criticized your work. Help me to see every way I am unique and lovely. You are such an amazing creator, Lord! I trust the work of your hands, and I believe you have always known what is best for me. Your handiwork behooves the plans you set out in front of me! Help me today and every day to always be grateful and thankful for the way you crafted me so perfectly. I am in awe of your workmanship.

In Jesus' name, amen.

Replace It!

When lies enter your thoughts today, immediately replace them with...

"I Am God's Workmanship, His Handiwork."

Write It!

"I am God's workmanship, His handiwork."

Have you ever wished to be different in any way or coveted another person's characteristics or attributes?

What amazing ways about yourself equips you for the work you have been called to?

What false belief will you let go of today?

Day Four

I Am Chosen of God, Holy and Dearly Loved

"For we know brothers and sisters loved by God, that he has chosen you."

1 Thessalonians 1:4

False Belief

I am unworthy.

For many, it's not easy to think of oneself as chosen and holy. Most of the time I don't feel worthy to be called chosen, holy, and dearly loved by God. I am grateful these labels are not contingent on anything we have done and everything to do with what Christ so sacrificially did on the cross. His love replaces our ungodliness with his holiness. Sometimes, I imagine God lowering his hand from heaven and placing it gently on my head to say, "I have called you by name. You are mine."

"But now, this is what the LORD says— he who created you, Jacob, he who formed you, Israel: 'Do not fear, for I have redeemed you; I have summoned you by name; you are mine.'" Isaiah 43:1

As believers we are set apart, but we are all at different places in our sanctification. With the help of the Holy Spirit, we can become more compassionate, kind, humble, gentle, and patient, although, different personalities allow some of these traits to come more naturally to some than others.

"Therefore, as God's chosen people, holy and dearly loved, clothe yourselves with compassion, Kindness, humility, gentleness and patience." Colossians 3:12

A few years ago, I learned this lesson while I unfairly judged another Christian at my church. From my perspective at that time, this lady was not very kind to me and others. A friend lovingly pointed out that God was not done working in her life just as he was still working in mine.

That was a huge awakening for me that really opened my eyes. My biggest obstacle to overcoming my critical nature was that I put everyone in the same box. I had to learn that living in judgment of others causes a lot of hurt feelings and resentment for all.

Being able to see that everyone is a work in progress, including myself, and that because God made us all unique, our responses and reactions to situations will of course differ.

This realization has helped me to be able to let go of grudges and hurt feelings. I have become less critical and judgmental with help from the Lord. Fortunately, he is still working on me, and I am grateful he continues to show me where I need improvement.

"For by one sacrifice he has made perfect forever those who are being made holy." Hebrews 10:14

Scripture References:

1 Thessalonians 1:4, Isaiah 43:1, Colossians 3:12, Hebrews 10:14

Lord, help me!

Father, I pray you continue to sanctify me in the ways of your son, Christ Jesus. Help me to show more compassion, kindness, humility, gentleness, and patience with others and myself. Thank you, Lord, for choosing me and loving me. I am eternally grateful that I am made holy because of you.

In Jesus' name, amen.

Replace It!

When lies enter your thoughts today,
immediately replace them with...

"I Am Chosen of God,
Holy and Dearly Loved"

Write It!

Is there a certain struggle in your life that generates a false belief that you are unworthy to be chosen by God?

In what ways do you see the Lord sanctifying you through that struggle?
What false belief will you let go of today?

Day Five

I Am Part of the True Vine

"I am the true vine, and my Father is the gardener."

John 15:1

False Belief

I am defeated.

Many years of my life were lived as a one-footed Christian. I use that term to describe how I was lukewarm with one foot in and one foot out. Within a few short years after being baptized, I started to drift back to old ways of looking for acceptance from former friends, men, and a lot of alcohol. I lived my life this way for a long time and it was exhausting; attending church on Sunday, only to find myself drinking at a club the following weekend, sometimes waking up in places that would make me cringe with shame. I suppose at the core of this behavior was that God was not enough for me and the approval of others mattered more. That is a hard sentence to type, but it was obviously true.

"I know your deeds, that you are neither cold nor hot. I wish you were either one or the other! So, because you are lukewarm—neither hot nor cold—I am about to spit you out of my mouth." Revelation 3:15-16

Thinking back to the day I was baptized and the excitement I felt about my new Christian life, I would not have believed anyone if they had told me the roller coaster of ups and downs I would go through. In my early twenties, I reluctantly started attending a Christian church with a friend from work where eventually I was baptized. At that time, I had not been to church since grade school but eventually said yes to her weekly invitations, obliging her, and not knowing my life was about to change.

I began learning about God in a completely different way than I had ever heard before. I never knew about having a relationship with him. There was always a reverence for God but he seemed so far removed from my life and unapproachable. Week after week, I started to heal with each message from the pulpit and could not contain the emotions that produced the big tears.

"He heals the brokenhearted and binds up their wounds."
Psalm 147:3

A hunger stirred in me to know God's word. He wooed me with songs, and I was so eager to share about all the ways he was changing me. As I started talking more and more about God with family and friends, my naivety was exposed.

What? I thought everyone believed in God. This sweet time in my life started to spiral downward as family chastised me and friends teased me. Calls from friends became few, and I was left without a place to fit in and without support. This is when the tug of war on my soul seemed so persistent. As God wooed me, Satan was convincing me that a Christian life was weird and lonely. I was unarmed as a baby Christian, so Satan won a battle or two; but then God took him down.

"Put on the full armor of God, so that you will be able to stand firm against the schemes of the devil." Ephesians 6:11

Apart from Christ, we are not who we are intended to be and cannot experience the full measure of life God has for us. Sure, we can experience moments of temporary pleasure and short-term happiness but that is not what life is about. Seeking pleasure and happiness only leaves us unfulfilled and always looking for more; the next best thing. It is a never-ending and agonizing cycle that, when apart from Christ, may not be recognizable for the one caught up in it.

"I am the vine; you are the branches. If you remain in me and I in you, you will bear much fruit; apart from me you can do nothing."
John 15:5

I love the illustration of Christ as the vine and God as the gardener. We are of course the branches that, if removed from Christ, cannot produce any good fruit; we are dead. His act of love on the cross for us establishes our true and eternal life.

Fortunately, my story does not end in defeat and my days of being a one-footed Christian are gone. Our Father, the gardener with his pruning shears, has always had his hand on me. He began a good work in me and will see it through to completion. My ups and downs and back and forth ways have taught me that seeking to know Christ and remaining in him far outweigh any earthly pleasure.

Also, I now know my relationship with him is the only one that will ever completely satisfy and fulfill me. I am only my true self with both feet in and am incredibly full; it feels like I am home.

"...being confident of this, that he who began a good work in you will carry it on to completion until the day of Christ Jesus."
Philippians 1:6

Scripture References:

John 15:1. Revelation 3:15-16. Psalm 147:3. Ephesians 6:11. John 15:5. Philippians 1:6

Thank you for all the ways you are pruning me and helping me bear the best fruit. Show me the ways I can help grow your kingdom and be a voice of truth for someone else. Lord, I ask that you would never remove your hand from me and always woo me back when I start to turn my back to you. Thank you for your unconditional love and forgiveness and for always taking me back into your arms.

Replace It!

When lies enter your thoughts today, immediately replace them with...

"I Am a Part of the True Vine."

Write It!

"I am a part of the true vine."

Was there a time when you turned back to your old life before knowing Christ?

Are you back in his arms now? How does it feel to be home or what will it take for you to return?

What false belief will you let go of today?

Day Six

I Am the
Salt of the Earth

"You are the salt of the earth. But if the salt loses its saltiness, how can it be made salty again? It is no longer good for anything, except to be thrown out and trampled underfoot."

Matthew 5:13

False Belief

I am not good enough.

Every day on my route to work I would pass a man who sat on a bench at the corner of a busy intersection. In his right hand he carried a megaphone and around his neck a sign condemning everyone to hell. He shouted the truth from the bench but the message felt completely void of love, based on the tone of his voice and the angry look on his face.

"If I speak in the tongues of men and of angels, but have not love, I am only a resounding gong or a clanging cymbal. If I have the gift of prophecy and can fathom all mysteries and all knowledge, and if I have a faith that can move mountains, but have not love, I am nothing."
1 Corinthians 13:1

At the time, I was already a believer but my Christian walk languished. I remember feeling shame and failure as I passed by this man, who shouted I was going to hell. I don't see where his shouting was effective in the trajectory of my life but maybe it planted an unconscious seed. He obviously impacted me enough to remember him as I write about him now.

Personally, I do not condone shouting by megaphone as a method of winning souls for the kingdom, but I do know God can use anyone and any situation for his glory. I also do not know this man's heart but God does.

"All a man's ways seem right to him, but the LORD weighs the heart."
Proverbs 21:2

As believers, we are to be the salt to those around us. We are to offer love, compassion, and generosity to the corrupt world around us and thwart evil in the world; by being the "salt," we slow down destruction. We convey hope to those around us by displaying Christ's love. Our saltiness encourages others to "come taste and see that the Lord is good."

"Taste and see that the LORD is good; blessed is the one who takes refuge in him." Psalm 34:8

Salt has many important roles; it is a preservative, it heals wounds, and is an important electrolyte in the body. It improves flavor, symbolizes purity, value, durability, and loyalty.
Salt is in every cell of our body, and it also helps flush out toxins.

Salt is so valuable that it was even used as currency once upon a time. It is no wonder why the disciples of Christ are referred to as salt of the earth. Followers of Christ salt the earth with the goodness of God.

So what happens if our flavor turns bland? We are no longer palatable. Rather than working to grow the kingdom, we work against it. Losing our saltiness can refer to much but what comes to the forefront of my mind is hatred —hatred for those who are different from ourselves, hatred for those who have different types of sin than we do, hatred for those who may have wronged us. Hatred is such a dangerous weapon used by Satan in his demonic schemes. Instead of embracing hate in our hearts, keeping our eyes on Jesus and following his example are the keys to remaining salty!

"Can that which is tasteless be eaten without salt, or is there any taste in the juice of the mallow?" Job 6:6

Father, enhance my saltiness so I may be the best ambassador for you that I can be. Help me to witness to others with love in my heart.

Remove the parts about me that judge others and keep me from festering hate. Thank you for the help of the Spirit that keeps my eyes turned to Jesus and convicts me when I start to follow the ways of this world rather than the ways of my savior.

Replace It!

When lies enter your thoughts today,
immediately replace them with...

"I Am the
Salt of the Earth."

Write It!

"I am the salt
of the earth."

What situation or person wrongly made you feel like a failure in your walk with Christ?

What are three
ways you
have salted
the world with
goodness?

What false belief
will you let go
of today?

Day Seven

I Am the
Light of the World

"You are the light of the world...
...let your light shine before others, so that they
may see your good deeds and glorify your
Father in heaven."

Matthew 5:14-16

False Belief

I am out of control.

*E*ight months pregnant and feeling the size of a horse, my hormones were raging! Those who know me will testify to my easy-going nature and ability to not let miniscule things such as inconsiderate drivers on the road ruffle my feathers.

However, the pregnancy hormones took over, and I became a force to be reckoned with. It only got worse when my sweet angel was born and in the backseat. Momma Bear was on alert, ready to attack anything or anyone that dared come close to harming us.

The wakeup call came when I found myself chasing down a truck tailing too close, then passed me with reckless abandon. I honked and yelled for him to pull over, not having a clue what I would do if he actually did. My daughter was not in the car when this went down but I had a sticker on the back of my car alerting those around me a baby was on board! That sticker needed to go, as it triggered me into being on "full alert."

The real moment that sent a dagger straight to my heart came when my two-year old yelled out, "Arrrrh mommy monster!" Apparently someone pulled out in front of me or got too close and I responded in a less than "Christ-like" fashion.

The veil was jerked from my eyes, and I felt compelled to invite the Lord into this mess, to take away the rage. Out of control, I needed to stop this barbaric behavior. I remember thinking I was glad for not putting that ichthus on the back of my car; this is not the action of a Christ-follower. God brought to light this part of me filled with anxiety and desperately needed sanctification. I needed to trust we were in his hands.

"Search me, God, and know my heart; test me and know my anxious thoughts. See if there is any offensive way in me, and lead me in the way everlasting." Psalm 139:23-24

Light gives us the ability to see clearly and exposes everything in full detail; as Christians we are in the spotlight. The world watches our actions and reactions, the way we treat others, how we give, and if our walk matches our talk. That is a lot of pressure to be under; but God said, "Let there be light," so we are given this opportunity to shine for Him.

"And God said, "Let there be light," and there was light." Genesis 1:3

Ways to be the light need not be complex. Speak kindly to the waitress serving you, offer the homeless man a couple bucks or spare change, greet the grocery store clerk, value and respect those the Lord has placed in your path. You may lift someone's spirit who is going through a rough time or you may actually lead someone to Christ! Jesus said the world will know we are his disciples by the way we love people.

"By this everyone will know that you are my disciples, if you love one another." John 13:35

We all have off days and can be judged unfairly by others, especially by those who do not know our hearts. It is impossible to respond perfectly in every circumstance when we are not perfect people. Giving grace to others is a great way to receive grace when we need it and another way to offer light to the world.

"Let us then approach God's throne of grace with confidence, so that we may receive mercy and find grace to help us in our time of need." Hebrews 4:16

"Blessed are the merciful, for they will be shown mercy." Matthew 5:7

Scripture References:

Matthew 5:14-16, Psalm 139:23-24, Genesis 1:3, John 13:35, Hebrews 4:16, Matthew 5:7

I know I will make mistakes and I am not perfect, but please help me to remember its important to be a good ambassador for you and someone is always watching. Lord, I know it is an imperative role to have and I thank you for helping me with this every day. Thank you, Lord, that someone may see my deeds or actions and come to know you more.

Replace It!

When lies enter your thoughts today, immediately replace them with...

"I Am the Light of the World."

Write It!

"I am the light of the world."

Can you think of a time you responded to a situation when your emotions were high and you felt out of control?

Write about a
time that you
responded to the
Holy Spirit's nudge
to make a change
in behavior?

What false belief
will you let go
of today?

Day Eight

I Am Loved

Neither height nor depth, nor anything else in all creation, will be able to separate us from the love of God that is in Christ Jesus our Lord.

Romans 8:39

False Belief

I am unloved.

Oh to be loved! This verse from Romans 8 has always been a favorite of mine. Just reading the words alone makes me feel important and loved. I remember the first time I read this verse—the only words my mind could form at that moment were just "wow!"

This was one of those times that makes me wonder if I had only known then what I know now how different things may have been. Would I have allowed myself to be used, disrespected, or dismissed so easily by others? If I had known I was the daughter of the King, would I have expected others to value me as so? Would I value myself as so?

"I will be a Father to you, and you will be my sons and daughters, says the Lord Almighty." 2 Corinthians 6:18

Now, speaking as a royal who has come to know her position, I definitely expect things would have been different. Of course I can't say that I am never tempted to fall back to false beliefs, but my roots are deeper now. I may bend from time to time but I will not break. Satan may persist in his insidious ways to convince me otherwise or remind me of past sin but my weapons against him are immeasurably stronger. I have God, the creator of all things, on my side, and now because I read it and know it, his word is on my side, too.

"What, then, shall we say in response to these things? If God is for us, who can be against us?" Romans 8:31

"Put on the full armor of God, so that you can take your stand against the devil's schemes." Ephesians 6:11

Some think of love as a feeling. I think it can be felt at times but love is an action. It is patient, kind, it does not envy or boast, and it is not proud. You know the verse recited at 90 percent of wedding ceremonies and for good reason. All of the actions included are vital to a strong marriage, as well as any other relationship.

Love is patient, love is kind. It does not envy, it does not boast, it is not proud. It does not dishonor others, it is not self-seeking, it is not easily angered, it keeps no record of wrongs. Love does not delight in evil but rejoices with the truth. It always protects, always trusts, always hopes, always perseveres. 1 Corinthians 13: 4-7

I know it may not be so easy to read words and immediately feel love, especially when life experiences have shown you differently. It may be that the actions of others have been cruel, abusive, damaging, or traumatic. Or you may be a woman whose grip on your past sins keeps you from allowing yourself God's grace and forgiveness. You may feel unworthy. Each of us has a story, and for some, that story is a hard one to tell. We don't feel loved and have shut the door to the possibility of being loved.

I wish I could provide answers for the suffering endured but instead I would like to take a shot at offering hope. We have endured, made it through, lived to see another day, and with another day comes triumph. We are overcomers, loved unconditionally by God.

"For everyone born of God overcomes the world. This is the victory that has overcome the world, even our faith." 1 John 5: 4-5

I, too, have had to cling to him in all those moments of worthlessness. When I could only muster the words "Lord, help me," he always came to my rescue. He pulled me from a dark place, lifted me up, and gave me purpose; a reason to live my life with hope.

When we accept Christ as our savior, we get to be forever in the presence of God and take in his affection; that is what Christ did for us! Nothing in creation is more powerful than its creator, just like there is no sin past, present, or future that outweighs the forgiveness and love of God. He desires that we fully accept his love and grace.

"The Lord, the Lord, the compassionate and gracious God, slow to anger, abounding in love and faithfulness..." Exodus 34:6

Scripture References:

Romans 8:39. Corinthians 6:18. 1 Corinthians 13: 4-7. 1 John 5:4-5. Exodus 34:6

I accept your love and am grateful for it! Thank you,
Jesus, for the most profound act of love ever displayed.
We praise you and love you.
Lord, help us to release the pain from those who have
hurt us. Replace any hurt feelings that we are holding
on to with hope for our future. Draw near, Lord, at
those times when we can't seem to move past the pain.

In Jesus' name, amen.

Replace It!

When lies enter your thoughts today, immediately replace them with...

"I Am Loved."

Write It!

"I am loved."

What are the circumstances that you find it difficult to accept that you are loved?

Knowing that
you can never loose
the love
of our Heavenly
Father, can you
accept that love
is not based on
anything you do
or have done?

What false belief
will you let go
of today?

Day Nine

I Am Christ's Friend

"I no longer call you servants because a servant does not know his master's business. Instead I have called you friends, for everything I have learned from my Father, I have made known to you."

John 15:15

False Belief

I don't have enough friends.

We call many our friends but in actuality very few really fit the bill. Having a large group of friends has never fit my personality, and I am sure has cost me some "cool person" points. If I am honest, I have sometimes thought I did not measure up to fit in any group long term. There were opportunities in high school to insert myself in groups of "friends," and I would do this on occasion but I just didn't like it. It seemed I had to pretend to be someone I was not in order to continue in the group.

As an adult, I am comfortable with admitting that I prefer a handful of great friendships over the favor of a group of people. If we are fortunate, the ones we call friends are frequently part of our days. In my current stage of life, I am a mom of a six-year-old, who works a full-time job outside of the home. Moments with friends do not come as often as I would like but when I do have the opportunity to spend time with a good friend, it ignites my spirit!

"Every good and perfect gift is from above, coming down from the Father of the heavenly lights, who does not change like shifting shadows." James 1:17

God blesses us by bringing people into our lives to enhance it. We are built for relationships, and thrive when we feel accepted, understood, and encouraged. He uses our relationships with others to lift us up, speak truth into our lives, and sometimes for rebuke. Our friendships with others are also a reminder to loosen up, enjoy life, and laugh. I treasure time with my best friend as an absolute gift.

"A friend loves at all times, and a brother is born for a time of adversity." Proverbs 17:17

Christ extends this type of relationship to us and invites us to spend time with him. He completely understands everything we face today. When we feel no one understands, he does. He has been betrayed, ridiculed, abused, left alone in his time of need, and deeply grieved.

He even faced death, knowing there was no other way to fulfill
God's will.

"Greater love has no one than this: to lay down one's life for one's
friends." John 15:13

There have been times I have envisioned Jesus sitting beside me
holding my hand. This has helped me through some low moments. He
tells me he is working it out and he will be with me through it all. He
will never leave us. Instead, he offers us a friendship that surpasses
this world. Oh what a friend we have in Jesus!

"The Lord himself goes before you and will be with you; he will never
leave you nor forsake you. Do not be afraid; do not be discouraged."
Deuteronomy 31:8

Scripture References:

John 15:15, James 1:17, Proverbs 17:17, John 15:13, Deuteronomy 31:8

Lord, help me!

Thank you for never leaving my side and always
being a friend to lean on. I love all the moments
we get to spend together.
Help me to find more of these moments throughout
my day. I long to be with you, Lord, and am grateful
that no matter the circumstance, you will always
be there. Its encouraging to know that I am fully
understood by you.

In Jesus' name, amen.

Replace It!

When lies enter your thoughts today,
immediately replace them with...

" I Am Christ's Friend "

Write It!

I am
Christ's Friend

Was there a time in your life that you felt no one understood what you were going through?

How did your relationship with Jesus get you through that moment?

What false belief will you let go of today?

Day Ten

I Am a Citizen of Heaven

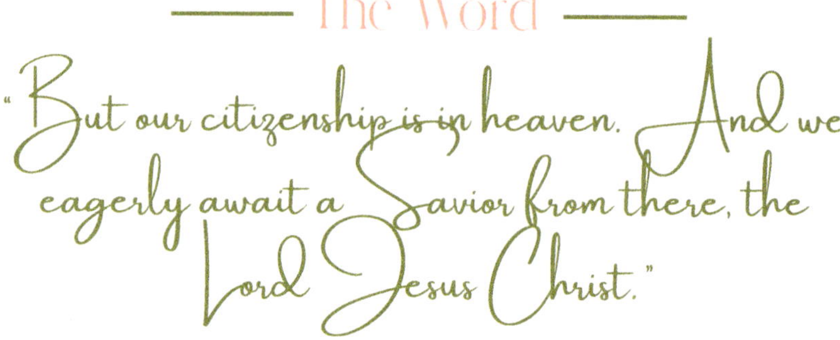

Philippians 3:20

False Belief

I am lost.

Maranatha! O Lord, come! The first time I ever heard this word and its meaning, my first thought was everything but "yes, Lord, come!" I began to list in my mind all the things I hadn't done yet and all the places I hadn't been. "Not yet Lord, I still need to get married first and then I really want to travel and oh can you just wait until ..." It's obvious I really did not understand what awaits us; it is far above anything our minds can put together.

"However, as it is written: "What no eye has seen, what no ear has heard, and what no human mind has conceived" the things God has prepared for those who love him." 1 Corinthians 2:9

We are in this world but not of it, a realization I had to grasp to get my mind focused on the things above. The Lord changed my heart and gave me a longing to be with him, to know him. He showed me through his word that he is the prize! Heaven is not what we win for being good Christians; we could never earn it. God with us for all eternity is his gift to us.

"What we have received is not the spirit of the world, but the Spirit who is from God, so that we may understand what God has freely given us." 1 Corinthians 2:12

And even though my mind can't possibly get there, I still attempt to picture myself in heaven chatting with Jesus. Knowing the gift of heaven is in my future compels me to press on no matter my circumstance. Not only that but what Christ endured to secure my spot there stirs my enthusiasm to be about His will for me. The thought of hearing his voice say, "Well done good and faithful servant, " forms a throat lump of emotion I can't really articulate.

"His master replied, 'Well done, good and faithful servant! You have been faithful with a few things; I will put you in charge of many things. Come and share your master's happiness!" Matthew 25:21

As a citizen of heaven we will always be somewhat unsettled here in our temporary home because we belong with the Lord. I'm grateful to know this now and am ready and eager for the Lord to return. Maranatha!

"And God raised us up with Christ and seated us with him in the heavenly realms in Christ Jesus" Ephesians 2:6

Scripture References:

Philippians 3:20, 1 Corinthians 2:9, 1 Corinthians 2:12, Matthew 25:21, Ephesians 2:6

Keep my mind set on things above. How wonderful it will be to finally be with you for all eternity; Oh glorious day! Father, redirect my mind when I start to covet the things of this world and remind me that this is my temporary home. Thank you for preparing a place for me in your Kingdom. I long to be forever in your presence.

In Jesus' name, amen.

Replace It!

When lies enter your thoughts today, immediately replace them with...

" I Am a Citizen of Heaven "

Write It!

I am a citizen
of heaven

What earthly treasure do
you need to put less value
on to be more eternal minded?

What are you most excited about when you think of Heaven?

What false belief will you let go of today?

113

Day Eleven

I Am a Member of the Body of Christ

"Now you are the body of Christ, and each one of you is a part of it."

1 Corinthians 12:27

False Belief

I am flawed.

Something must be wrong with me! No one else seems to make excuses to escape noisy situations where there is endless chatter. Everyone else laughing but I am on the verge of screaming and running away. This has been a familiar feeling of mine for many years and still is. The difference now is that I understand why I am this way and that it's a completely normal reaction for introverts.

I am pleased to tell you that I am an introvert. This is not because I believe being an introvert is more or less desirable than my extroverted friends, it's just that until just a few years ago I was ashamed of this trait about myself. I tried to mask the fact that I needed to be alone sometimes. After becoming more open about it, I discovered that many feel this same way.

"We have spoken freely to you, Corinthians, and opened wide our hearts to you. We are not withholding our affection from you, but you are withholding yours from us. As a fair exchange—I speak as to my children—open wide your hearts also."
2 Corinthians 6: 11-13

When you make yourself vulnerable, you will learn a lot about others. It is not just introverts who feel this way; many extroverts struggle with their inclinations, too. Rather than exalt one disposition over the other, let's celebrate our unique ways! After all, God made us the way we are, and we are all an important part of the body of Christ! The purpose we have been granted by God requires the traits he gave us. The apostle Paul explains how our differences work so beautifully together in 1 Corinthians 12:12-20:

"Just as a body, though one, has many parts, but all its many parts form one body, so it is with Christ. For we were all baptized by one Spirit so as to form one body—whether Jews or Gentiles, slave or free—and we were all given the one Spirit to drink. Even so the body is not made up of one part but of many.

Now if the foot should say, "Because I am not a hand, I do not belong to the body," it would not for that reason stop being part of the body. And if the ear should say, "Because I am not an eye, I do not belong to the body," it would not for that reason stop being part of the body. If the whole body were an eye, where would the sense of hearing be? If the whole body were an ear, where would the sense of smell be? But in fact God has placed the parts in the body, every one of them, just as he wanted them to be. If they were all one part, where would the body be? As it is, there are many parts, but one body."

Reading this illustrates just how necessary each member of the body truly is. When Satan attempts to convince us that our worth is less than another's, we can think back to this example and know that if we cease working for the kingdom, the rest of the body of Christ is weakened.

"For we are members of his body." Ephesians 5:30

Scripture References:

1 Corinthians 12:27, 2 Corinthians 6: 11-13, 1 Corinthians 12:12-20, Ephesians 5:30

Thank you for all the unique ways you created me. I know that my personality fits your will for me perfectly. Help me to appreciate the differences in others knowing they are perfectly created too. I am honored to be a member of the body of Christ. Thank you for this gift of community and purpose.

When lies enter your thoughts today,
immediately replace them with...

" I Am a Member of
the Body of Christ"

Write It!

When have you thought or
what circumstance made
you feel like you were flawed?

What is your part in the body of Christ? This is most likely what others always tell you they appreciate about you.

What false belief will you let go of today?

Day Twelve

I Am an Heir of God

"Because you are his sons, God sent the Spirit of His Son into our hearts, the Spirit who calls out "Abba Father". So you are no longer a slave, but God's child; and since you are his child, God has made you also an heir."

Galatians 4:6-7

False Belief

I am poor.

In high school, my best friend who lived down the street and I would walk our neighborhood several times after dinner. We had to be sure to burn off any calories we had just consumed! Eventually we made our way across the tracks to the "rich people's" subdivision. It sounds so cliché but this neighborhood of massive houses was literally across the tracks and up the hill from where we lived.

We loved to imagine that we lived in one of those houses and spent many nights under the stars camped out by the pond in the middle of the subdivision. It was so fun to envision what our lives would be like if we were among these fortunate residents or an heir to their wealth. My view of the world was much different then.

"For everything in the world—the lust of the flesh, the lust of the eyes, and the pride of life—comes not from the Father but from the world."
1 John 2:15-17

There was never a time when my family didn't have food to eat, clothes to wear, and a place to sleep. My sisters and I were well provided for and taken care of but there was no extra money for brand name clothes, vacations, or eating out. We had everything we needed but we were far from being called heiresses of a large inheritance. Thankfully, what the Lord offers for those of us who love him far surpasses any earthly amount of wealth.

"But seek first his kingdom and his righteousness, and all these things will be given to you as well." Matthew 6:33

An earthly inheritance is typically reserved for members of one's family; those related to the grantor are the ones to receive what will be passed to them. Those who do not belong to the family, should not expect to be a recipient of anything; it is the same for the family of God.

To be an heir of God is to be in the family of God. We are ushered into his family the very moment we accept and believe in the one he sent to save us from his wrath. When we trust Christ as our savior, our inheritance is secure and will never perish, fade, or vanish. It cannot be lost!

We inherit life eternal, forever in communion with our Lord, in a place that has no sorrow or tears. Because of his grace, God sees Jesus when he looks upon us. Hallelujah!

"For he chose us in him before the creation of the world to be holy and blameless in his sight. In love he predestined us for adoption to sonship through Jesus Christ, in accordance with his pleasure and will—" Ephesians 1:4

This is the amazing gift he offers but not all receive it. Some will reject Jesus as the son of God, refuse a part in God's family, and live a life void of any relationship with him. My heart aches for those who still presume heaven is part of their story but refuse Jesus. Only God knows who, if someone died today, may hear the words, "Depart, I knew you not." God knows our hearts.

"Not everyone who says to me, 'Lord, Lord,' will enter the kingdom of heaven, but only the one who does the will of my Father who is in heaven. Many will say to me on that day, 'Lord, Lord, did we not prophesy in your name and in your name drive out demons and in your name perform many miracles?' Then I will tell them plainly, 'I never knew you. Away from me, you evildoers!' Matthew 7:21-23

Our Father who created us, loves us and continues to shower us with his grace, love, and forgiveness, desiring his creation to accept the inheritance he has for us. He will not force it upon us though, it has to be received. He chooses us but we must choose him, too, to become his heir. Don't delay!

"Here I am! I stand at the door and knock. If anyone hears my voice and opens the door, I will come in and eat with that person, and they with me." Revelation 3:20

Scripture References:

Galatians 4:6-7, 1 John 2:15-17, Matthew 6:33, Ephesians 1:4, Matthew 7:21-23, Revelation 3:20

I am an Heiress of the largest inheritance that can be obtained. Thank you for adopting me in to your Kingdom. Help me not to covet riches on earth that belong to others. Instead, let me always be grateful for the many blessings you shower upon me daily. Thank you Father for such an amazing gift to look forward too.

In Jesus' name, amen.

Replace It!

When lies enter your thoughts today, immediately replace them with...

" I Am an Heir of God "

Write It!

What material possessions
have become an idol in your
life now or in the past?

Why are treasures in Heaven much more valuable than earthly possessions?

What false belief will you let go of today?

Day Thirteen

I Am a Temple

"Don't you know that you yourselves are God's temple and that God's Spirit dwells in your midst?"

1 Corinthians 3:16

False Belief

I am helpless.

Hi, my name is Jenny, and I have an eating disorder. I use food in every other way above the nourishment of my body. I am a compulsive eater, I eat my feelings instead of feeling them and turning to God. I am a food addict.

After writing the words above, I stared at them for three days. I felt paralyzed and unable to write any further. I prayed, cried, and stared some more. But then the Lord spoke to my heart the realization I needed. I am NOT an eating disorder. Instead, I am a temple of the Holy Spirit. I smiled, closed my eyes, and thanked him. I may have also said out loud, "Back in your face, Satan!"

So much guilt and shame is tied to our bodies. Sometimes our physical appearances can be a mirror for the sin in our lives; it is so for me. I have been known to avoid my reflection mostly because I felt I wore my sin on exhibit for the world to see. It is a heart-piercing reminder of a time that I know I am forgiven for but still haunts me. Satan likes to use this to bring me down.

Another lie I often fend off is that when people meet me they only see the extra eighty pounds my frame carries. A quick assessment of my weight might be that I eat too much and should just stop it. A deeper look reveals much more.

Having a food addiction is like alcoholism and may even be trickier to overcome. Alcoholics in recovery avoid alcohol altogether, whereas food addicts face food several times a day.

I have suffered food issues most of my life but had always been able to keep off the extra weight until about ten years ago when Satan attacked hard. I fell into both an alcohol and food addiction simultaneously. My life spiraled out of balance. Rather than clinging to the Lord, I turned further from him.

Looking back, it is easy to see how a life far from God can result in addiction. My alcohol abuse started with me being a workaholic. I worked seven days a week, long hours and in a toxic environment. My position in the company was extremely stressful and taxing on the brain. In addition, my boss would explode into an offensive rant without a moment's notice.

I drank every night. My work addiction had now become an alcohol addiction, and I felt like I continually needed a buzz from alcohol to deal with life. There were times I worked from home and drank all day, watching the clock to justify a glass of wine earlier and earlier each day. When I did go to the office, I often went hung over. My hangover craved the grease from fast food. As a result, I gained 130 pounds from the day I met my husband ten years prior.

"Do you not know that your bodies are temples of the Holy Spirit, who is in you, whom you have received from God? You are not your own.
1 Corinthians 6:19

One Christian in the office saw me. She looked through my sin and saw the pain. She didn't say anything but prayed regularly for me. I am grateful the Lord placed her there at such a pivotal moment. She made the difference by intervening on my behalf to the Lord when I could not do it for myself.

"Carry each other's burdens, and in this way you will fulfill the law of Christ."
Galatians 6:2

"Therefore confess your sins to each other and pray for each other so that you may be healed. The prayer of a righteous person is powerful and effective." James 5:16

The Lord healed me and delivered me from alcohol. This was a miraculous act of God; there is no other way to explain it. There is redemption in addiction, especially when we learn that he is the ultimate source of our fulfillment. Only he can satisfy the soul completely, and nothing else is required.

His Spirit never left me, I just ignored him for so long. But through his relentless love, he assured me I am his, a precious temple!

"And the prayer offered in faith will make the sick person well; the Lord will raise them up. If they have sinned, they will be forgiven."
James 5:15

Scripture References:

1 Corinthians 3:16, 1 Corinthians 6:19, Galatians 6:2, James 5:16, James 5:15

There is nothing that can satisfy me more than knowing you. Thank you for always taking me back when I look to other things for fulfillment. Thank you for your forgiveness and help me to always chose you above everything. Remind me that I am much more valuable that my struggles and loved by the creator of all things. Thank you for your Spirit that lives inside me and helps me battle all that comes against me.

Replace It!

When lies enter your thoughts today, immediately replace them with...

" I Am a Temple "

Write It!

What have you struggled
with that was damaging
to your temple?

Knowing you have the help of the Holy Spirit, how does that affect your plan of attacking this struggle?

What false belief will you let go of today?

Day Fourteen

I Am A Holy Partaker in A Heavenly Calling

" Therefore, holy brothers and sisters who share in the heavenly calling, fix your thoughts on Jesus, whom we acknowledge as our apostle and high priest."

Hebrews 3:1

False Belief

I am deprived.

My husband has some unique interests and hobbies, which is just one of the things I love about him. This past year he has become a bee farmer, and we were recently able to extract our first crop. I have learned a lot about bees this past year and they are truly amazing creatures. They know precisely their role in the hive and perform their duties without question. Everything works like a well-oiled machine. For us humans, it's a bit more complex.

"There is a time for everything, and a season for every activity under the heavens..." Ecclesiastes 3:1

Much of my life has been spent searching for purpose, and I have come to realize our heavenly calling is to fully know and strive to be like Jesus. When I finally grasped this, everything else lost its luster.

Nothing on Earth is better than knowing him and experiencing him daily. Also, nothing is worth the risk of losing that. Like many of you, I only wish I had known this sooner. I would have saved myself much heartache. Thankfully, part of God's plan is to take our trials and use them for his glory! I love that he always offers redemption... always.

"I press on toward the goal to win the prize for which God has called me heavenward in Christ Jesus." Philippians 3:14

"Nevertheless, each person should live as a believer in whatever situation the Lord has assigned to them, just as God has called them..." 1 Corinthians 7:17

We were created to glorify the Lord, to worship him. Our calling in life is not to be happy, get married, have a good job with decent insurance and benefits, take family vacations, and the list goes on. None of these things are bad, and many are blessings from God or answers to prayer...rather, typically, we do not place them in the right order of importance.

Above all things, we are made to honor the Lord with our lives by accepting Jesus as our savior, follow his example and tell others about him. We are called to grow the kingdom.

"For in him all things were created: things in heaven and on earth, visible and invisible, whether thrones or powers or rulers or authorities; all things have been created through him and for him." Colossians 1:16

Honestly, this mindset did not always sit well with me. I thought I deserved and was entitled to more. What about my happiness and comfort? My heart saw things differently, and my desires were self-serving. As I grew closer to the Lord, my prayers started to change. The more time I spent with him in prayer and in his word, my eyes began to open. He changed me from the inside out..

When I first read Hebrews 3:1, the familiar hymn by Helen Lempel settled in. As I hummed "Turn your eyes upon Jesus, look full in His wonderful face, and the things of earth will grow strangely dim, in the light of His glory and grace," I thought about how true these lyrics really are. We navigate this world the best by turning our eyes to Jesus.

One day these troubles will all fade away for good. I don't always remember to do so but those times when I am faced with a hard situation or feel hurt, thinking about my promise in Jesus minimizes the feelings I am having in that moment. The hurt feelings are temporary but his love and gift of salvation are forever.

"He has made everything beautiful in its time. He has also set eternity in the human heart; yet no one can fathom what God has done from beginning to end." Ecclesiastes 3:11

Scripture References:

Hebrews 3:1, Ecclesiastes 3:1, Philippians 3:14, 1 Corinthians 7:17, Colossians 1:16, Ecclesiastes 3:11

I desire to keep my eyes fixed on you, there is nothing in this life that compares. Thank you for the gift of Heaven and help me to keep my thoughts on the treasure that awaits me there. You are the prize Lord and I can't wait to be with you there. Continue to mold me to love like you and remind me that true joy is found in putting my life is in your hands.

Replace It!

When lies enter your thoughts today,
immediately replace them with...

" I Am A Holy Partaker in
A Heavenly Calling"

Write It!

What have you prioritized
above your Heavenly calling?

How does shifting your focus to Jesus change your perspective on things in life you have not yet obtained?

What false belief will you let go of today?

Day Fifteen

I Am United to the Lord

"But whoever is united with the Lord is one with Him in spirit."

1 Corinthians 6:17

False Belief

I am a failure.

At the tail end of 2019, knowing absolutely nothing about online business, I started a Christian women's gift shop. I had so many exciting dreams about what it could turn into but no idea what the following year would bring. What began as a fun way to use my creativity to bring the Word to women, quickly became all about the dollar bills to be made.

Many businesses thrived in the challenges the 2020 coronavirus pandemic brought, but mine did not. Still, I pressed on the entire year. I had lost sight of my mission, and it became a major self-pity wallowing extravaganza that I had lost so much money.

Distracted and discouraged, I took on a mindset of defeat. I quit for almost a full year despite the many women I had built relationships with during in that time. I know I must have let them down! Finally I chose to surrender all my plans. In that moment, he blessed me with the most amazing vision. If only I would have listened to him sooner, but I'm so grateful his mercies are new every morning.

"Because of the Lord's great love we are not consumed, for his compassions never fail. They are new every morning; great is your faithfulness." Lamentations 3:22-23

Our sinful nature separates us from God but he unites us back to himself through Jesus. You may have heard it said that people are inherently good; for those who buy into that, I must bring the truth. Inherently we are driven by the flesh, self-seeking and sinful...all reasons we rely on Jesus to deliver us to righteousness. If we were naturally good, we would not need a savior. The apostle Paul struggled with this very thing and wrote about it to the Christians in Rome.

"As it is, it is no longer I myself who do it, but it is sin living in me. For I have the desire to do what is good, but I cannot carry it out." Romans 7: 17-18

"Thanks be to God, who delivers me through Jesus Christ Our Lord! So then, I myself in my mind am a slave to God's law but in my sinful nature a slave to the law of sin." Romans 7:25

So deeply nested in our hearts is this sinful condition that only a life fixated on Christ has any promise of turning away from it. Freedom from sin and fellowship with the Lord is our reward. Proclaiming Jesus as Lord unites us to God in this way and invites His Spirit to reside within.

"But the Advocate, the Holy Spirit, whom the Father will send in my name, will teach you all things and will remind you of everything I have said to you." John 14:26

Even so, we can rebel and choose to ignore the Spirit which is where the power of prayer comes to our rescue. He will help us and provide a way out from the sin we struggle with. For me, the struggle can be discouraging at times, and I become extremely disappointed in myself.

"Do not quench the Spirit." 1 Thessalonians 5:19

It can be tempting to wallow in that moment of falling to my nature instead of basking in the forgiveness Jesus has already given. Satan can strike hard when we are down, and he thrives on our pain, reminding us of failures like they are on a repeat reel in our minds. His goal is to keep us down deep in self-pity and rob us of our joy.

Since take #2 of my ministry started in January 2022, I have dealt with many bouts of illness. Not just feeling under the weather but sickness that has kept me nonfunctioning for weeks at a time. Some may say coincidence. but I know I am in a spiritual battle. The war has already been won, and we know who reigns victorious. Although Satan has been relentless in his efforts against me, the Lord's power in me is so much stronger! I am united with the Lord who fights for me, so I am able to continue on the mission. Remember, he will do the same for you.

Scripture References:

1 Corinthians 6:17, Lamentations 3:22-23, Romans 7: 17-18, Romans 7:25, John 14:26, 1 Thessalonians 5:19

Let me hear you clearly; change my desires to line up with your will for my life. Thank you for your discipline that is shaping my character and growing my faith. Father, I trust your master plan and my role in it. Thank you for your forgiveness for the times I have forsaken your will for my own selfish desires. Help me to remember that your ways and thoughts are so much higher than mine.

Replace It!

When lies enter your thoughts today, immediately replace them with...

" I Am United to the Lord "

Write It!

I am united to the Lord

Do you remember a time when you trusted your own abilities and ideas above God's?

How much easier did things work out for you when you trusted God's perfect plan?

What false belief will you let go of today?

Day Sixteen

I Am One of God's Living Stones Built in Christ as a Spiritual House

"You also, like living stones, are being built into a spiritual house to be a holy priesthood, offering spiritual sacrifices acceptable to God through Jesus Christ."

1 Peter 2:5

False Belief

I am alone.

Can you picture a stone mason examining his materials and carefully selecting each one as he determines them deserving of being used in his work? He reaches for a stone that is unique from the others, varying in color and texture. He tosses it aside. It would cause too much attention to itself and disrupt the pattern.

In this imagery, the stone mason represents the world as it rejects Jesus and the truth he brings. Jesus most assuredly disrupts the pattern of conformity and not only stands out but looks completely different. He is the only way to the Father, our savior, and the cornerstone of our faith. This is not a popular message with the world but for the believer, we know that without him there is no hope.

"Do not conform to the pattern of this world, but be transformed by the renewing of your mind. Then you will be able to test and approve what God's will is—his good, pleasing and perfect will."
Romans 12:2

A cornerstone of a building marks the direction in which it will be built. It is the first stone to be laid, and all other stones are stacked from its orientation. Remove this stone and the whole system crumbles. Just as it is so with Jesus in or out of our lives; it is not hard to see how this is being played out all around us today. Jesus has been removed from just about every public venue, and we are now seeing those consequences.

For the Christian, we are his living stones being built up to reflect him. As we work on our sanctification, we continue to look more like him each day. With Jesus being the cornerstone in our lives, he gives us boldness and confidence to battle anything that would attempt an attack on our souls.

"I can do all this through him who gives me strength."
Philippians 4:13

I like to picture us as God's children, living stones, coming together to form a strong fortress not allowing anything through that would cause us to stumble. United in truth and love, this spiritual house continues to strengthen in faith. What used to seem as sacrifices become more easily given.

"As iron sharpens iron, so one person sharpens another."
Proverbs 27:17

In my life, community was not always important or desired. Not surrounding myself with mature Christians is a large part of why I fell away from the church for a significant amount of time. With one leg in my faith and one leg in the world, I craved a relationship with God less and less, and few in my circle to care.

This lesson fell on me very slowly but assuredly I began to understand why we are created for relationships and community. Comparing ourselves again to stones, individually scattered here and there, we have no real impact. But together, we can be something quite magnificent, having Jesus as the cornerstone, full of power! Hallelujah!

"And let us consider how we may spur one another on toward love and good deeds, not giving up meeting together, as some are in the habit of doing, but encouraging one another—and all the more as you see the Day approaching." Hebrews 10:24-25

Scripture References:

1 Peter 2:5. Romans 12:2. Philippians 4:13. Proverbs 27:17. Hebrews 10:24-25

Lord, help me!

Keep me in community with other believers so we may encourage and strengthen one another. Father, you are wise and good; you made us to thrive in relationships. Thank you for the body of Christ that prays for me, cares about the posture of my heart, and destination of my soul. I am so grateful for the believers you have put in my path. Help me to cherish and nurture these precious relationships you have blessed me with.

In Jesus' name, amen.

Replace It!

When lies enter your thoughts today, immediately replace them with...

" I Am One of God's
Living Stones Built in Christ
as a Spiritual House"

Write It!

Describe your community
of believers that you have
now or had in the past.

How does
or would
community
strengthen and
enhance your
life?

What false belief
will you let go
of today?

Day Seventeen

I Am a Saint

"To the church of God in Corinth, to those sanctified in Christ Jesus and called to be his holy people, together with all those everywhere who call on the name of our Lord Jesus Christ— their Lord and ours:"

1 Corinthians 1:2

False Belief

I am a bad person.

Without really knowing the true meaning, my first response to being called a saint is that I am far from it. When we think of someone as a saint, a person who is perfectly pleasing in all circumstances comes to mind. However, its significance is much more meaningful than how a person reacts to a tough situation.

Being called a saint means that we are his! We belong to God and are followers of Christ; we are faithful servants dedicated to his service and called to be his holy people. In light of this proper definition, do you feel differently about being called a saint? For most of us, I imagine the answer would be not always.

"So then you are no longer strangers and aliens, but you are fellow citizens with the saints, and are of God's household,"
Ephesians 2:19 ESV

As a baby Christian barely emerged from the baptismal, I had some things wrong. The part I had right was that I believed God loved me, sent his son to die for me, and that I needed and believed him to be my savior. Aside from that, I did not know God's word or what it meant to follow Christ.

Much like the Pharisee who prayed about how good he was to God rather than the tax collector asking for mercy, I began to unlovingly judge those around me. This was not Christ- like at all and sure to cause damage to relationships both horizontal and vertical. Rather than seeing the person God created and loved, I saw the sin and somehow deemed myself better. I justified my sins not as despicable on an artificial scale created by me.

"But the tax collector stood at a distance. He would not even look up to heaven, but beat his breast and said, 'God, have mercy on me, a sinner. I tell you that this man, rather than the other, went home justified before God. For all those who exalt themselves will be humbled, and those who humble themselves will be exalted."
Luke 18:13-14

What I grew to learn is that perfection is not required from the lover of our soul. We will sin, make mistakes, and fumble just as our nature drives us to. Thank goodness God does not disqualify us for that. We simply call upon the name of the Lord, and we are sanctified. We take our transgressions to him and he is faithful to forgive.

"If we confess our sins, he is faithful and just and will forgive us our sins and purify us from all unrighteousness."
1 John 1:9

God's word has taught me about the human condition, what he did to rectify our sin, and how to love and forgive those in my life because he does the same for me. This privilege of forgiveness is for the saints, believers in our Lord Jesus Christ. Experiencing his grace, mercy, and love is most known to us when we fail to be untarnished. He is the perfect one so we do not have to be. Praise God!

"For by one sacrifice he has made perfect forever those who are being made holy." Hebrews 10:14

Scripture References:

1 Corinthians 1:2. Ephesians 2:19 ESV . Luke 18:13-14. 1 John 1:9. Hebrews 10:14

Thank you for always being faithful to forgive.
Remind me to pass along the same grace to others as
you so freely give to me. Help me to remember that
there are not levels of sin; you hate all sin equally. As
much as you hate sin, you still love me though I do
not deserve it. Thank you for your unending love
and for calling me one of your saints.

In Jesus' name, amen.

Replace It!

When lies enter your thoughts today,
immediately replace them with...

" I Am a Saint "

Write It!

I am a saint

When did you judge
someone else's sin as
greater than your own?

How does it feel to be called a saint knowing God forgives all who call upon him and accept Jesus as Lord ?

What false belief will you let go of today?

Day Eighteen

I Am a Stranger to This World in Which I Temporarily Live

"Dear Friends, I urge you as foreigners
and exiles to abstain from sinful desires
which wage war against your soul"

1 Peter 2:11

False Belief

I am a coward.

hen I started a new job several years ago, it was clear to me and my coworkers that I did not belong. The talk was foul, and the conversations were almost hostile against whomever was being defamed in the moment. The quarters were tight, and I was extremely uncomfortable. Despite my reluctance, I attempted to learn more about those who surrounded me for so many hours of the day.

Unlikely friendships were formed with some as a result while others reaffirmed their initial dislike of me. Although I was completely content with not fitting in with this particular group, it still felt lousy to be so obviously excluded. I did a lot of praying and self-talk during this time to remind myself of whom I belonged to. It was a bona fide exercise of renewing my mind daily.

In some moments of weakness I gave in to my fleshly desire to be liked, speaking and acting like someone who did not know God. I always immediately regretted it and felt ashamed, asking God to help me to be a better ambassador the following day.

I'm still unclear whether I sincerely intended to positively impact my coworkers and plant Godly seeds. And I'll likely never know whether or not I influenced them at all. To a few, I was a shoulder to cry on and an ear to listen; some I prayed for unbeknownst to them and some because they asked me to, while certain others unmercifully ridiculed me and did as much as possible to keep me as an outsider.

This experience, as much as it was tough to endure, was a far distant comparison to the persecution that Jesus and the apostles suffered. Even so, it reminded me of a few things that all of us who are Christians should keep close to our hearts and at the forefront of our minds.

Act like a follower of Christ—Assuredly we will interact with unbelievers in this life, and they are paying close attention to our words, our reactions, our moods, and everything about us, hoping to discredit our Lord.

While we know sin is inevitable in all our lives and that Jesus forgives those who accept him as their Lord, the unbeliever does not have this knowledge. It becomes imperative we exude the fruits of the Spirit, asking God to help us reflect his character to the world. Perfection is not possible, but we can strive to be more like Christ with each day, prayerful that the good they see in us will bring glory to God.

"Whoever claims to live in him must walk as Jesus did." 1 John 2:6

Fill up your cup and renew your mind—It's impossible to have a holy mindset when we take in all things unholy. The power our minds have over our overall well-being is incredible and the reason Satan continually whispers his lies. We become susceptible to those lies when we ignore the power of the Holy Spirit and consume only secular things. How can we renew our minds to think more like Christ when we are flooded with the wrong information?

We have the Word of God to fill our minds with all the truth needed to navigate life in this temporary home. Take it in, meditate on it, and memorize it. Transformation of our minds and hearts will be inevitable and clearly evident to those who know us.

"Finally, brothers and sisters, whatever is true, whatever is noble, whatever is right, whatever is pure, whatever is lovely, whatever is admirable—if anything is excellent or praiseworthy—think about such things."
Philippians 4:8

Pray and keep the faith—Prayer is everything but often the last thing we think to do. In reality, though, it is a gift from God that he desires to spend time with us. Prayer is an act of obedience, a worshipful demonstration of love and trust. Also, prayer allows us an incredible time to rest in his presence. The most powerful and effective weapon against Satan and his schemes is prayer. For all these reasons, we are instructed to do so without ceasing and unequivocally as a way to remain faithful.

"For our light and momentary troubles are achieving for us an eternal glory that far outweighs them all. So we fix our eyes not on what is seen, but on what is unseen. For what is seen is temporary, but what is unseen is eternal."
2 Corinthians 4:17-18

Know Who You Are — Jesus was invariably opposed, ridiculed, and mocked each time he spoke publicly. Yet, he never faltered or seemed offended in any way. In times when I have felt rejected, I found comfort in knowing that Jesus experienced rejection, too. Knowing he can empathize with my struggle provides great comfort, and I stay in awe of his ability to remain strong in those times of direct opposition.

Even though he is God, in his time on Earth he was fully man.
Jesus knew exactly who he was. He was completely confident in his identity, knew his purpose, and had no inkling of doubt about it. His only concern was to do the will of his Father, and the opinions and comments from others did not matter. I pray for this level of self-assurance for all Christians. Imagine the boldness we could possess when we know exactly who we are and whose we are!

"And we know that in all things God works for the good of those who love him, who have been called according to his purpose. " Romans 8:28

Forgive me for those times that I cower under pressure and put what others think above what you think. Help me to be brave and bold when talking about you and never to be ashamed of my faith. Remind me that my relationship with you matters more than any brief moment of acceptance from my peers. Thank you, Lord, that you are the same yesterday as you are today and that I can never loose your love.

Replace It!

When lies enter your thoughts today, immediately replace them with...

" I Am a Stranger
to This World "

Write It!

Was there ever a time that you downplayed your faith to others?

Describe a time when you were bold sharing your faith.
What false belief will you let go of today?
195

Day Nineteen

I Am Righteous and Holy

"You were taught, with regard to your former way of life, to put off your old self, which is being corrupted by its deceitful desires; to be made new in the attitude of your minds; and to put on the new self, created to be like God in true righteousness and holiness."

Ephesians 4:24

False Belief

I am a jerk.

at (insert expletive)," she said, looking directly at me. I should have seen that coming right before it happened, and in that moment I knew her words were true. This encounter smashed the cherry on top of the day I had been having, and everything else bad that had happened sent my emotions tumbling out of control.

When I pulled into a spot up front at Thornton's gas station and ran in to buy a drink, I was tired, overworked, and not in the best of moods. Looking forward to my Coke Zero, I came out of the store to find someone parked too close to my car on the driver's side. Even if I were not a fat "beep" there was no way a human could fit in the space they left me.

The car had dark tinted windows but I could tell a person was in the driver's seat. With a smile on my face, I skipped over to their side, tapped on the window, and politely asked if they could make some more room for me to get into my car. At least that is what I should have done... but it went down a bit differently. I hate to admit that my first response was anger and my actions reflected that. I stood in front of that car waving my finger at them, demanding they move.

Where was the love of Christ in me at this moment? Far from being like God, righteous and holy, I left the gas station, embarrassed and ashamed. I believe this was another one of those pivotal points in time that God used to show me my heart's condition. It was apparent I needed to open myself up to change. I prayed for the Holy Spirit's guidance and help that I would become slow to anger next time I was faced with a sticky situation.

"For those who are led by the Spirit of God are the children of God."
Romans 8:14

God has given us the gift of the Holy Spirit for such a time as this. If I am relying on myself to be righteous and holy, I am certain to fail. When this incident occurred I was not attuned to the Spirit, not in the Word, and really not praying much. My attention was swayed, and I was forced to look at myself. Like you, I am made in the image of God, a daughter of the King and holy. Therefore, I should act like it.

"Since we live by the Spirit, let us keep in step with the Spirit."
Galatians 5:25

The only way to put off the old and put on the new is to pray for that.
I believe it's a process that gets better with practice and comes from
a changed heart. We must first know what the new self is, want to put it
on, and pray for help to live out our faith this way. Everything points back
to reading the Word and prayer; it's essential. If we want to see God move
in our hearts, this is how to open the flood gates of heaven. This is how we
stay righteous and holy. Read. Pray. Change.

"Create in me a pure heart, O God, and renew a steadfast spirit within me."
Psalm 51:10

"I will give you a new heart and put a new spirit in you; I will remove from
you your heart of stone and give you a heart of flesh."
Ezekiel 36:26

Let me always be attuned to the leading of the Spirit.
Let my actions reflect the characteristics of the one living
inside me. Lord, you are powerful and wise; remind me
to lean on you for strength in all situations. Thank you
for your love and forgiveness in these moments that my
actions leave me feeling ashamed. Continue to sanctify
me more each day to resemble your son Jesus.

In Jesus' name, amen.

Replace It!

When lies enter your thoughts today, immediately replace them with...

" I Am Righteous and Holy "

Write It!

I am righteous and holy

Describe a time when you
acted before thinking through
the consequences of
those actions.

When did the Holy Spirit help you through a tough moment that otherwise would have ended unfavorable.

What false belief will you let go of today?

Day Twenty

I Am Reconciled to God

"All this is from God, who reconciled us to himself through Christ and gave us the ministry of reconciliation: that God was reconciling the world to himself in Christ, not counting people's sins against them. And he has committed to us the message of reconciliation.

2 Corinthians 5:18-19

False Belief

I am a poseur.

Just before the pre-launch of this journal, imposter syndrome started to creep in. Satan loves these moments of weakness, and he has been lingering, waiting to strike. He immediately goes for the jugular with the procession of lies sure to plant major seeds of doubt.

"Who do you think you are? You're nobody, and no one is going to want your book. You are going to embarrass yourself with all the bad reviews. Stop all this foolishness while you still can!" he relentlessly whispers.

There is another voice telling me to keep going, so I carry on knowing I am about my Father's work.

Then the enemy slaps me in the face with the gargantuan of lies: "Look at all you have done, you have no right sharing God's word with others with YOUR past. Everyone is going to laugh at you. Stop trying to be someone YOU ARE NOT!" This one is tougher to combat.

"Submit yourselves, then, to God. Resist the devil, and he will flee from you."
James 4:7

Earlier this year I attended a life-changing Christian retreat for women. It was powerful, full of symbolism and imagery. The exercise that was most impactful for me was what I call the circle of lies. Half of the women formed a circle in the middle of the room while seated in chairs, and the other half of the women stood behind them. The lesson began when the women standing, each equipped with a different lie, whispered the lie into the ear of the seated women in front of them. They moved around the outside of the circle spreading their lie to each woman seated.

"Be alert and of sober mind. Your enemy the devil prowls around like a roaring lion looking for someone to devour. Resist him, standing firm in the faith, because you know that the family of believers throughout the world is undergoing the same kind of sufferings." 1 Peter 5: 8-9

This was really emotional and brought many of us to tears as some lies are ones we continually tell ourselves and believe. As daunting as this was, it was only the first part.

However, the second part was much brighter. In the same manner the lie was spoken, the women now spoke the truth to each one seated. The mood in the room instantly changed when they were filled with honest truth and love.
The incredible thing is that I do not remember the lie I was given to spew but I do remember the truth I spoke. I told each woman there is nothing they can do to lose God's love for them.

"Though the mountains be shaken and the hills be removed, yet my unfailing love for you will not be shaken nor my covenant of peace be removed," says the Lord, who has compassion on you." Isaiah 54:10

I am standing on that truth now as I continue to write and share. My past sins are forgiven because of the sacrifice of Jesus, and I am reconciled to God. He made everything right again, He has restored our relationship with the Father and remembers our sin no more.

To believe Satan negates the death of Christ. Jesus died an agonizing death on a cross for us to have victory over this world and the father of lies. We owe it to him to believe him; that is what I am choosing, and that is the message I am sharing. True love, God's kind of love, created a path to redemption.

"This is how God showed his love among us: He sent his one and only Son into the world that we might live through him. This is love: not that we loved God, but that he loved us and sent his Son as an atoning sacrifice for our sins. Dear friends, since God so loved us, we also ought to love one another."
1 John 4:9-11

Scripture References:

2 Corinthians 5:18-19, James 4:7, 1 Peter 5: 8-9, Isaiah 54:10, 1 John 4:9-11

Lord, help me!

I choose to believe you. Help me when I am being tempted with lies; may I continue to believe your Word instead. Thank you that no weapon formed against me shall prosper. I am grateful for the power that lives in me, the gift of the Holy Spirit. Greater is He who lives in me than he who is in the world. Let these truths always be in the forefront of my mind.

In Jesus' name, amen.

Replace It!

When lies enter your thoughts today, immediately replace them with...

" I Am Reconciled to God "

Write It!

Is there a particular lie
from Satan that halts your
progress for the Kingdom?

How does it feel knowing you only need to resist believing in a lie and Satan will be commanded to flee from you?

What false belief will you let go of today?

215

Day Twenty One

I am Hidden with Christ

"For you died, and your life is now hidden with Christ in God..."

Colossians 3:3

False Belief

I am insincere.

"Word of Life" is a song sung by Jeremy Camp and one you might catch me hiking up the volume and head-bobbing to in the car. There is a lyric in the song that draws out the most emotion in me: "You called me out of the grave so I can live like I've been changed!"

I think this phrase is the secret sauce, the key to approaching life. An attempt to put this feeling in words might be described as deep gratitude, a heart that longs to change. Sometimes I'm overcome with sadness that I don't measure up.

"Whoever claims to live in him must live as Jesus did." 1 John 2:6

My walk with Christ is stronger than it has ever been but I regret that it has taken twenty-five years for it to completely click in my brain. That is the number of years since I publicly proclaimed my faith in Jesus as my savior through baptism. In that time I have surrendered my life but also taken it back a few times. It is a daily battle for us all; we choose to walk in love and faith or fear and lies.

"You will seek me and find me when you seek me with all your heart." Jeremiah 29:13

Early in my Christian life, I prayed the Lord would never leave me and that he would always bring me back to him if I ever strayed. How I was inclined to pray such a prayer at that time I am not sure, but the Lord reminds me of this prayer each time he has wooed me back. Always in awe of how he does it, I find myself questioning how I ever abandoned him.

"..Being confident of this, that he who began a good work in you will carry it on to completion until the day of Christ Jesus." Philippians 1:6

I want off the rollercoaster of this Christian life I have led. Instead, I desire steady feet on solid ground with a life fully committed to the Lord, completely trusting his will and a heart to love and forgive like Christ. When Jesus says we should die to ourselves it's because that is how we come alive, exchanging our flawed hearts for ones that bears his resemblance.

"For to me to live be Christ, and to die is gain." Philippians 1:21

Dying to self is a hard concept to grasp. The first time hearing it I did not like the sound of that. "What am I supposed to give up?" I thought this meant to relinquish my hopes and dreams, stop caring about my appearance, and only participate in church activities. No, the Lord gave us our hopes and dreams and many gifts unique to each one of us. We don't stop being who he created us to be. We bring glory to him by putting those gifts to work to grow the kingdom.

"Every good and perfect gift is from above, coming down from the Father of the heavenly lights, who does not change like shifting shadows."
James 1:17

This Christian walk is all about the heart. We are to die to or let go of our natural propensity to anger, greed, anxiety, selfishness, and such things. Instead, God calls us to come alive in patience, generosity, peace, and love! Mere human predisposition to sin will not achieve this flawlessly like Christ does, but still we follow. We follow and he changes us, thus becoming more like him. We are hidden with Christ because God sees Jesus when he looks at us.

"Follow God's example, therefore, as dearly loved children and
Walk in the way of love, just as Christ loved us and gave himself up
for us as a fragrant offering and sacrifice to God."
Ephesians 5:1-2

Scripture References:

Colossians 3:3, 1 John 2:6, Jeremiah 29:13, Philippians 1:6, Philippians 1:21, James 1:17, Ephesians 5:1-2

Lord, help me!

Thank you for your sacrifice on the cross that so intensely demonstrates the profound love you have for me. What greater love could there ever be? You left the 99 and you chased after me. You have never left me and I praise you, Lord, for your perfect ways that always draw me back to you. Keep me in your care and remind me that I am a daughter of the Most High! I love you and trust you completely with my life.

In Jesus' name, amen.

Replace It!

When lies enter your thoughts today,
immediately replace them with...

" I am Hidden with Christ "

Write It!

I am hidden

with Christ

What song or scripture
creates deep emotions in you?
Why do you think that is so?

Describe the feeling of being hidden with Christ knowing that when God looks upon us, Jesus is who He sees.

What false belief will you let go of today?

About The Author

Jenny is a natural-born encourager and loves those around her to feel lifted up and loved. She is the founder of a ministry for women called Beautiful as YOU that has a core focus of cultivating confidence in Christian women.

She is a native of Kentucky, where she resides with her husband, John, daughter, Izzy, and their Aussie, Pepper Lou.

They are novice honey farmers and aspire to grow their apiary to a family business.

Some of Jenny's favorite things to do are spending her coffee time with Jesus in the morning, learning more about God's word, singing and dancing with her daughter, and fine dining with her hubby.

Jenny prefers meaningful conversations with a great friend over large groups of acquaintances. She is passionate about her calling to help women see themselves the way God sees them and expresses her creativity through the written word, drawing, and graphic design.

Hey, friend! If you are reading this page, this means you have purchased my very first devotional and prayer journal! Thank you isn't enough to express my gratitude. It means more than you know.

This is the first of many things to come as the Lord directs my steps. Stay tuned to what comes next at www.beautifulasyou.com and be sure to add your email address so I can keep you updated.

I pray you have been blessed after diving into conquering negative self-talk and exchanging that for truth the past twenty-one days. It isn't magic. Change doesn't happen overnight, and you'd better believe the enemy lurks close by. However, you now have some tools to fight back: prayer and the Word of God! I see Satan shaking in his boots already, assuming he is a boot-wearing devil.

Enough about him, to God be the glory! My hope and prayer is this book has blessed you enough that you will share this knowledge with other struggling women. There are two effective ways you can do that. To begin, you can simply add your review of this book on Amazon or my website so it will become more visible to others who need it. Secondly, you can purchase a copy for someone God has laid on your heart time and time again over the reading of this book.

Thank you for letting me share my heart and struggles with you. It has been both therapeutic and challenging at times, but oh so very worth it.

With Love and Hugs,

Jenny K

Repeat After Me...

I Am a New Creation

I Am a Child of God

I Am God's Workmanship, His Handiwork

I Am Chosen of God, Holy and Dearly Loved

I Am Part of the True Vine

I Am the Salt of the Earth

I Am the Light of the World

I Am Loved

I Am Christ's Friend

I Am a Citizen of Heaven

I Am a Member of the Body of Christ

I Am an Heir of God

I Am a Temple

I Am a Holy Partaker in a Heavenly Calling

I Am United to The Lord

I Am One of God's Living Stones

I Am a Saint

I Am a Stranger to this World

I Am Righteous and Holy

I Am Reconciled to God

I Am Hidden with Christ

Stay In Touch

There is more where this came from. I would love for you to stay in touch with all the new and exciting things going on at Beautiful as You!

Visit www.beautifulasyou.com

For Free Resources,

Upcoming Books and Courses, to

Join a Private Community For Christian Women,

plus much more. Go check it out!

For

Prayer and Support

or to say hey,

Email Me:

JennyK@beautifulasyou.com

www.ingramcontent.com/pod-product-compliance
Lightning Source LLC
Chambersburg PA
CBHW080900160726
48000CB00009B/2798